Classic Recipes of
LEBANON

Classic Recipes of
LEBANON

TRADITIONAL FOOD AND COOKING
IN 25 AUTHENTIC DISHES

GHILLIE BAŞAN

PHOTOGRAPHS BY JON WHITAKER

LORENZ BOOKS

This edition is published by
Lorenz Books,
an imprint of Anness Publishing Ltd,
108 Great Russell Street,
London WC1B 3NA

www.lorenzbooks.com;
www.annesspublishing.com

If you like the images in this book and
would like to investigate using them for
publishing, promotions or advertising,
please visit our website
www.practicalpictures.com for more
information.

Publisher: Joanna Lorenz
Editor: Joanne Rippin & Helen Sudell
Designer: Nigel Partridge
Production Controller: HelenWang
Recipe Photography: Jon Whitaker

The image on the front cover is of
Chickpea and Bulgur Salad with Mint,
page 20.

A CIP catalogue record for this book is
available from the British Library

PUBLISHER'S NOTE

Although the advice and information in this
book are believed to be accurate and true
at the time of going to press, neither the
authors nor the publisher can accept any
legal responsibility or liability for any errors
or omissions that may have been made nor
for any inaccuracies nor for any loss, harm
or injury that comes about from following
instructions or advice in this book.

These recipes were originally published as
part of a larger volume, *Lebanese Food &
Cooking*.

PUBLISHER'S ACKNOWLEDGEMENTS

The Publisher would like to thank the
following agencies for the use of their
images. Alamy: p6, p8 bottom left, p10
bottom left. Istock, p9.

COOK'S NOTES

Bracketed terms are intended for American
readers. For all recipes, quantities are given
in both metric and imperial measures and,
where appropriate, in standard cups and
spoons. Follow one set of measures, but
not a mixture, because they are not
interchangeable.

Standard spoon and cup measures are
level. 1 tsp = 5ml, 1 tbsp = 15ml, 1 cup =
250ml/8fl oz. Australian standard
tablespoons are 20ml. Australian readers
should use 3 tsp in place of 1 tbsp for
measuring small quantities.

American pints are 16fl oz/2 cups.
American readers should use 20fl oz/2.5
cups in place of 1 pint when measuring
liquids.

Electric oven temperatures in this book are
for conventional ovens. When using a fan
oven, the temperature will probably need to
be reduced by about 10–20°C/20–40°F.
Since ovens vary, you should check with
your manufacturer's instruction book for
guidance.

The nutritional analysis given for each
recipe is calculated per portion (i.e. serving
or item), unless otherwise stated. If the
recipe gives a range, such as Serves 4–6,
then the nutritional analysis will be for the
smaller portion size, i.e. 6 servings. The
analysis does not include optional
ingredients, such as salt added to taste.

Medium (US large) eggs are used unless
otherwise stated.

Contents

Introduction

Although a small country, Lebanon boasts a vibrant cuisine, richly influenced by its climate and geography. A narrow coastal strip winds its way along the edge of the warm Mediterranean, with high mountains to the east, behind which lies the fertile Bekaa Valley, the main source of much of Lebanon's food. Considered by many to be Arab food at its best, most Lebanese dishes have their roots in pre-medieval times, and while there are significant differences between eating habits in the countryside and the modern cities, the ancient Lebanese tradition of hospitality is still expressed in a complex and exciting culinary culture.

Left: Sunset across the harbour and El Mina mosque, Tripoli, Lebanon.

Lebanese Cuisine

The food of Lebanon has its roots in two traditions: the peasant cooking of its fertile valleys and mountains, and the foreign influences found in the main cities and along the coast. Much of the sophistication of town cuisine can be attributed to the influence of the Ottoman Empire. In rural villages, ancient ways of preparing food are as they have been for centuries, with an emphasis on good quality food carefully cooked.

Above: Kibbeh can be made with meat, fish or vegetables.

Below: A bedouin woman making leavened bread.

Lebanese hospitality

The Arab tradition of hospitality and kindness is deeply ingrained in the psyche of most of the region's population. All Lebanese respect the family values and are deeply courteous and hospitable. When a host welcomes a guest it is normal to hear the words '*batyi, baytak*' ('my house is your house'). It is polite to offer food and drink to strangers and to invite them to partake of a meal.

When you enter into a Lebanese home, *kibbeh* is the traditional offering of hospitality. Often regarded as the national dish of Lebanon, its origin dates back to Mesopotamia. The word itself is derived from the Arabic verb meaning 'to form a lump or ball'. Although it has endless variations, it is most commonly a combination of minced (ground) lamb and bulgur wheat with grated onion and a variety of herbs and spices. There are also meatless versions employing lentils, vegetables or fish.

Food markets

Street markets are central to Lebanese life. From the sprawling cluster of permanent bazaars in the cities to the makeshift stalls of mountain villages the variety and abundance of fresh vegetables and fruit is overwhelming. The aroma of spices is ever-present, emanating from the spice stalls and the food vendors cooking with cinnamon, cumin, coriander, garlic, chillies, and the ubiquitous spice mix, zahtar.

Right: The rich, vibrant colours to be seen at a spice market stall, Beirut.

Feasts and Festivals

The Lebanese population is made up of roughly 59 per cent Muslims, 40 per cent Christians and 1 per cent other religions. With a tolerant attitude to the customs and cuisines of all faiths, the culinary year flows from one religious feast to another, incorporating the food traditions of both Muslim and Christian calendars.

Easter

This is the most important date of all on the Lebanese Christian calendar. On Good Friday, when devout Christians abstain from eating meat, a variety of bean,

Below: Easter procession through the streets of Beirut.

vegetable and lentil dishes are eaten, and a sour bulgur soup called *shoraba zingool*. The sourness of the soup is intended to remind Christans of the vinegar offered on a sponge to Christ. On Easter Sunday, large platters of *ma'amoul*, little semolina cakes stuffed with walnuts or dates, are offered to celebrate the end of Lent.

Eid al-Salib – St Helena's Day

One of the most celebrated feast days among the Christian communities is St Helena's Day, on 8 September. According to legend, Queen Helena, the Mother of the Roman Emperor Constantine, discovered the True Cross of the Crucifixion on a hillside above Jerusalem and demanded that fires be lit to spread the news. To celebrate this historical legend, fires are lit and fireworks light up the sky as Christians, and Muslims too, gather to dance and feast in the open air, and street vendors sell kibbeh and other delights late into the night.

Above: Savoury pastries are enjoyed as part of the Iftar meal.

Ramadan

This is the month when all Muslims fast between sunrise and sunset to mark the time when Muhammad experienced the revelation of the Qur'an. The first meal of the day, *suhur*, is prepared before dawn and is designed to fill the stomach for the daylight hours of fasting ahead, so it normally comprises a hearty soup and bread. *Iftar*, the second and last meal of the day, is consumed once the sun has gone down and is much more extensive, involving savoury pastries, meatballs or kibbeh, stuffed vegetables, and numerous sweet dishes, such as baklava, milk puddings, fruit compotes, and ma'amoul. Dates are always placed on the table at religious feasts to serve as a reminder that they were the only source of food for the Prophet Mohammad when he was fasting in the desert.

Eid al-Fitr
Once the month of Ramadan comes to an end, it is time to celebrate with a great deal of feasting over a three-day period. Two public holidays are set aside for Eid al-Fitr to allow everyone to eat and drink whatever they like.

Below: Dates always feature on a celebration table.

Eid al-Barbara
Another Christian celebration, that is also enjoyed by Muslims, marks the end of the harvest in late November. In a similar fashion to the Western traditions of Halloween, the children dress up, wear masks and devour sweet treats. In Lebanon, the traditional treat consists of bowls of kamhiyeh, wheat or barley sweetened with sugar and decorated with pomegranate seeds, which signify good luck and prosperity and is why they are often served to welcome visitors.

Above: Bowls of kamhiyeh are a traditional Christmas dessert.

Christmas
At Christmas Lebanese Christian communities generally celebrate with an exchange of gifts and a large family meal of roasted poultry or leg of lamb, on 25 December – just as Christians do in other parts of the world. The exceptions are the Armenians, who celebrate Christmas on 6 January, the Epiphany, with mounds of sticky *awamat* (deep-fried fritters bathed in honey).

Classic Ingredients

Here are some of the everyday ingredients that accompany vegetables, meat and fish to give the region's food much of its characteristic flavour.

Dairy products

Milk is rarely consumed on its own, instead it is used to prepare butter, clarified butter, yogurt, cheese and clotted cream. Yogurt forms an important part of the basic diet. It is served with rice and lentils or combined with herbs and garlic to form a dip or salad. For certain dishes, yogurt is strained through muslin (cheesecloth) to

Below: Bowls of olives are offered at mealtimes.

produce a dense cream-cheese consistency, which is ideal for mezze dishes.

Olives

White cheese and olives have provided sustenance for nomads of the Fertile Crescent since ancient times. A Lebanese table would be incomplete without a bowl of locally harvest olives, which are traditionally marinated in olive oil, thyme and lemon juice. Olive oil is used in every Lebanese meal, for cooking, dressing and enriching.

Bread

An essential component of every meal, leavened or unleavened bread is employed as a scoop, as a mop for soaking up the divine cooking juices, as a dipper to sink into a puréed garlicky mezze dish, and as an all-round table accompaniment. Since medieval times, bread has been prepared with barley, millet and wheat, but corn was introduced during the Ottoman era and became a feature of many village loaves.

Pickles

In Lebanon, pickling is the most popular method of preserving food such as fruit, vegetables and nuts. Classic combinations include pickled turnip with a few slices of beetroot (beet), or red cabbage with cauliflower, which produces a purple tint. Other pickles range from finely shredded cabbage together with apricots and green almonds to slices of aubergine (eggplant) wrapped around cloves of garlic and apricots and tied in a bundle with a thin ribbon of leek.

Individual pickles include jars of green beans, slim green chilli peppers, okra, onions, little unripe tomatoes, green walnuts, almonds and beetroot. Vine leaves, garlic cloves, coriander seeds, cinnamon sticks, allspice berries and thick, hot chillies are often added to the pickling jars, which are then filled with cider or white wine vinegar.

Right: Breaking bread together at a meal is central to the Lebanese way of life.

Above: Pomegranates are used in many Lebanese desserts.

With the Phoenician legacy of trading it is not surprising that herbs and spices play an important role in the cooking of the region. The following spices and flavourings are those you would find in a *munay*, the food cellar of a Lebanese home.

Carob molasses

This is a thick, dark syrup used to sweeten drinks, desserts and stews. A sweet paste made with carob molasses and tahini is often served with bread for breakfast, but it can also be served as part of a mezze by spiking it with crushed garlic, lemon juice and dried mint.

Pomegranate syrup

Unlike carob molasses, this is sour. The syrup is much coveted for salad dressings and marinades and is often drizzled over dishes for the exquisite fruity sour note it lends to them.

Sumac

This deep-red condiment is prepared by crushing and grinding the dried berries of a bush (*Rhus coriaria*) that grows wild in the mountains. It has a fruity sour taste and is often used as a substitute for lemons.

Mastick

This is the aromatic gum from a small evergreen tree (*Pistacia lentiscus*) that grows wild all over the Mediterranean region. The distinctive flavour is employed to enhance milk puddings, jams and ice cream.

Cinnamon

Originally from the Spice Islands, cinnamon is a pungent and warming spice, sold in stick or ground form and used in cakes, sweetmeats, stews and soups.

Above: Cinnamon sticks add warmth to stews and soups.

Coriander

Grown all over the Middle East and sometimes referred to as 'Arab parsley', fresh coriander (cilantro) leaves are fresh-smelling with a citrus taste. They are often added to stews and salads and work wonderfully with fish. The seeds have a peppery flavour and, when roasted, emit a nutty aroma.

Saffron

This attractive spice consists of the orange stigmas of the purple crocus (*Crocus sativus*). When soaked in water the stigmas impart a vivid yellow dye and a hint of floral peppery notes.

Cumin

These tiny seeds have a distinctive taste and, when roasted, they emit a delightful nutty aroma.

Garlic

This pungent herb has been used in the region since classical times.In rural villages, whole heads of garlic are often threaded on to skewers with strips of fat and grilled over an open fire.

Flat-leaf parsley

Parsley is used in many dishes, and is also served on its own to sharpen the appetite, to cut the

Below: Rose petals add a luxuriant touch to desserts.

Above: Fresh mint is refreshing and aids digestion.

spice, to cleanse the palate, or to freshen the breath. It is the principal feature of the national dish, tabbouleh, a parsley salad with bulgur wheat.

Mint

As this herb grows prolifically in the region it finds its way into many salads, dips, and soups.

Rose petals

These beautiful petals are used to garnish puddings, and rose-water, along with orange flower water, is used to flavour syrups for a variety of desserts. It is also the main ingredient of the sherbet drink *sharab al ward*.

Spice mixes

Throughout the Middle East you will come across a spice mix called Baharat (*below right*). In Lebanon this mix includes black pepper, coriander seeds, cumin, cinnamon, cloves, nutmeg and paprika.

Zahtar (*below left*) is the Arabic word for thyme. It is also the word for the spice mix which is sprinkled over bread, cheese, yogurt and salads and is a favourite seasoning for street vendors throughout the Fertile Crescent. It consists of dried thyme, ground sumac and salt.

Tastes of the Fertile Crescent

Lebanese cooking is reputed to be one of the most refined cuisines in the world. Its vibrant mix of culinary traditions is celebrated here with delicious mezze, salads and soups, hot snacks and fragrant pilaffs. Other recipes highlight a passion for tangy fish, sizzling meat, roast vegetables and wholesome bean stews. Finally, an irresistible selection of scented desserts, preserves and sweetmeats complete the evocative collection of recipes which represent the very best that Lebanese hospitality has to offer.

Left: Lamb, whether roasted, slow-cooked, or minced (ground) and made into kibbeh, is the favoured meat of most Lebanese cooks.

Fried Halloumi with Zahtar Hallum

Serves 2–4

250g/9oz plain halloumi cheese
45–60ml/3–4 tbsp olive oil
15ml/1 tbsp zahtar
lemon wedges and Lebanese flat
   bread, to accompany

*Available in Arab markets
and most supermarkets,
halloumi is a salty, firm white
cheese. In Lebanon, it is
made from cow's milk and
matured in whey, sometimes
combined with nigella
seeds, mint or thyme.
Generally, it is used in
savoury pastries, or slices
are grilled or fried and
served as a mezze dish.*

1 Rinse the halloumi under cold running water and pat dry with kitchen paper. Using a sharp knife, cut into thin slices.

2 Heat the oil in a heavy-based pan. Fry the halloumi slices for 2 minutes until golden, then flip over and fry the other side. Drain on kitchen paper.

3 Transfer the hot halloumi on to a serving dish and sprinkle with zahtar. Eat immediately, with some Lebanese flat bread and a squeeze of lemon.

COOK'S TIP
Serve the grilled halloumi straight from the pan, as it becomes rubbery when cool.

Smoked Aubergine Dip Baba ghanoush

Serves 4–6

2 large aubergines (eggplants)
30–45ml/2–3 tbsp tahini
juice of 1–2 lemons
30–45ml/2–3 tbsp strained yogurt
2 cloves garlic, crushed
small bunch of flat-leaf parsley,
    finely chopped
sea salt and ground black pepper
olive oil, for drizzling

1 Place the aubergines on a hot griddle, or directly over a gas flame or charcoal grill, turning them from time to time, until they are soft to touch and the skin is charred and flaky. Place them in a plastic bag for a few minutes to sweat and, when cool enough to handle, hold them by the stems under cold running water and peel off the skin. Squeeze out the excess water and chop the flesh to a pulp.

2 Beat the tahini with the lemon juice – the mixture stiffens at first, then loosens to a creamy paste. Beat in the yogurt and then, using a fork, beat in the aubergine pulp.

3 Add the garlic and parsley (reserving a little to garnish), season well with salt and pepper and beat the mixture thoroughly. Turn the mixture into a serving dish, drizzle a little olive oil over the top to keep it moist and sprinkle with the reserved parsley.

There are variations of this classic dish, also known as moutabal. Some cooks add chopped flat-leaf parsley or coriander (cilantro) while others lighten it with a little yogurt or lemon juice. The dish has a strong smoky flavour, which is best enjoyed with crusty bread, or pitta, to dip into it.

Chickpea and Bulgur Salad with Mint Safsouf

1 Place the bulgur in a bowl and pour over boiling water to cover. Leave to soak for 10–15 minutes, until it has doubled in volume.

2 Meanwhile, place the chickpeas in a bowl with the onion, sesame seeds and garlic and bind with the olive oil and lemon juice.

3 Squeeze the bulgur to remove any excess water and add it to the chickpeas with the parsley and mint. Toss well, season with salt and pepper to taste, and sprinkle the paprika over the top.

COOK'S TIP

To toast sesame seeds, heat a heavy frying pan, pour in enough seeds to just cover the bottom of the pan, then dry-fry over a low heat, stirring constantly, until the seeds turn golden brown. Remove from the pan immediately, and leave to cool. Alternatively, spread the sesame seeds on a baking tray and roast in a medium oven for a few minutes until golden brown. You need to keep a close eye on the seeds with either method, as they burn quickly.

Serves 4–6

150g/5oz/scant 1 cup fine bulgur, rinsed
400g/14oz canned chickpeas, drained and rinsed
1 red onion, finely chopped
15–30ml/1–2 tbsp toasted sesame seeds
2–3 cloves garlic, crushed
60–75ml/4–5 tbsp olive oil
juice of 1–2 lemons
bunch of flat-leaf parsley, finely chopped
large bunch of mint, coarsely chopped
sea salt and ground black pepper
5ml/1 tsp paprika, to garnish

This is a traditional village salad, using vegetarian ingredients that are readily available in the hills and valleys of Lebanon. The mixture can also be used as a filling for stuffed vine leaves or peppers and aubergines (eggplant) when meat is scarce. To prepare it as a salad, the ingredients are simply bound with olive oil and lemon juice and tossed with lots of fresh mint.

Chicken Wings with Garlic and Sumac Jawaneh

Serves 4–6

45–60ml/3–4 tbsp olive oil
juice of 1 lemon
4 cloves garlic, crushed
15ml/1 tbsp ground sumac
16–20 chicken wings
sea salt

1 In a bowl, mix together the olive oil, lemon juice, garlic and sumac.

2 Place the chicken wings in a shallow dish and rub the marinade all over them. Cover the dish and leave to marinate in the refrigerator for at least 2 hours.

3 Prepare the barbecue or preheat a conventional grill (broiler). Place the chicken wings on the rack and cook for approximately 3 minutes on each side, basting them with the marinade while they cook. Alternatively, preheat the oven to 180°C/350°F/Gas 4, place the chicken wings in an ovenproof dish, brush with the marinade and roast for 25–30 minutes.

4 When the wings are completely cooked, remove from the heat, sprinkle with salt and serve while still hot.

The aroma of chicken wings or drumsticks grilling over charcoal is always enticing, whether it is in a busy street market or in a clearing in the countryside. Great street and picnic food, these tasty chicken wings are best eaten with your fingers, straight from the oven, grill or barbecue.

Chicken and Saffron Broth with Noodles Shorbet al dajaj

1 To make the stock, place all the chopped vegetables in a large pan. Put the chicken on top of the vegetables, and add the parsley, peppercorns and allspice berries. Pour in just enough water to cover the chicken.

2 Bring the water to the boil, then reduce the heat, cover the pan and simmer gently for about 1½ hours, until the chicken is practically falling off the bones.

3 Lift the chicken out of the pan and set aside. Strain the stock into a fresh pan and discard the vegetables and spices.

4 When the chicken is cool enough to handle, pull the meat off the carcass. Discard the bones and reserve the dark meat for another dish. Tear the breast meat into thin strips, cover and keep warm.

5 Reheat the broth and stir in the saffron fronds. Bring the broth to the boil and add the noodles. Reduce the heat and boil gently for about 10 minutes until the noodles are cooked.

6 Add the chicken strips to the soup and heat through. Check the seasoning and add salt and pepper to taste. Pour the hot soup into individual bowls and sprinkle with a little parsley or mint before serving.

The more delicate Lebanese soups are generally served as an appetizer to a meal, whereas hearty soups made with vegetables and lentils, or meat and grain, may be served as a meal or snack on their own. This soup falls into another camp, as the cleansing broth with its floral notes of saffron is sometimes served as a palate cleanser between courses.

Serves 6–8
For the stock
2 celery stalks, with leaves, roughly
    chopped
2 carrots, peeled and roughly
    chopped
1 onion, roughly chopped
1 lean, organic chicken, about
    1.5kg/3¼lb, cleaned and trimmed
small bunch of parsley, roughly
    chopped
6 peppercorns
6 allspice berries

For the broth
generous pinch of saffron fronds
115g/4oz/1 cup vermicelli, or other
    noodles, broken into pieces
sea salt and ground black pepper
small bunch of fresh parsley or mint,
    finely chopped, to garnish

Creamy Red Lentil Soup with Cumin
Crema shorba al-adas

Serves 4

225g/8oz/1 cup red lentils
30ml/2 tbsp olive oil
40g/1½oz butter
10ml/2 tsp cumin seeds
2 onions, chopped
1 litre/1¾ pints/4 cups chicken stock
5–10ml/1–2 tsp ground cumin
sea salt and ground black pepper
1 lemon, cut into wedges, to serve
60ml/4 tbsp strained yogurt, to
    serve (optional)

1 Rinse the lentils and leave to drain. Heat the oil and butter in a large, heavy pan and stir in the cumin seeds. Cook, stirring, until they emit a nutty aroma. Add the onions, and when it begins to turn golden brown stir in the lentils.

2 Pour the stock into the pan and bring to the boil. Reduce the heat, cover the pan and simmer for about 30 minutes, topping up with water if necessary. Ladle the mixture into a food processor or blender and whizz to a smooth purée.

3 Return the soup to the pan to reheat, season with salt and pepper and ladle it into individual bowls. Dust with a little ground cumin and serve with lemon wedges to squeeze over. Add a spoonful of yogurt to each bowl, if you like.

Lentil and grain soups, often containing chunks of meat or vegetables, are common fare throughout the Middle East, but every so often you come across a simple, puréed soup, flavoured with a single ingredient such as mint or cumin, which is pleasantly refreshing.

Little Flat Breads with Thyme and Sumac
Manakakeish bil zahtar

Serves 4–6
7g/¼oz/2¼ tsp dried yeast
2.5ml/½ tsp sugar
300ml/½ pint/1¼ cups lukewarm
    water
450g/1lb/4 cups strong white (bread)
    flour, or a mixture of white and
    wholewheat flours
2.5ml/½ tsp salt
30–45ml/2–3 tbsp olive oil, plus
    extra for oiling
45–60ml/3–4 tbsp zahtar

*These spicy little breads are
very popular to eat as a
snack in the streets of Beirut
and at neighbourhood
bakeries, where they are
often chosen for breakfast.
They are also great as an
accompaniment to a
mezze spread.*

1 Dissolve the yeast with the sugar in a little of the water and leave to cream for about 10 minutes. Sift the flour with the salt into a bowl and make a well in the centre. Pour the creamed yeast into the well with the rest of the water and draw the flour in from the sides to form a dough.

2 Turn the dough on to a floured surface and knead well for about 10 minutes. Pour a drop of oil into the base of the bowl, roll the dough in it and cover with a damp cloth. Leave the dough to prove for 2 hours, until it has doubled in size. Preheat the oven to 200°C/400°F/Gas 6.

3 Mix together the olive oil and the zahtar to make a paste.

4 Knock back (punch down) the dough, knead it lightly, then divide it into about 20 pieces. Knead each piece into a ball, flatten and stretch it, and smear it with some of the paste. Place the breads on lightly greased baking trays and bake them in the oven for about 10 minutes, until golden brown. Serve them while still warm.

Spicy Bean Balls
Felafel

Serves 4–6

250g/9oz/1 cup dried broad (fava)
   beans, soaked overnight
115g/4oz/½ cup chickpeas, soaked
   overnight
10–15ml/2–3 tsp ground cumin
10ml/2 tsp ground coriander
1 red chilli, seeded and chopped
½ onion, chopped
1 red or green (bell) pepper, chopped
4 cloves garlic, crushed
small bunch of fresh coriander
   (cilantro), chopped
small bunch of flat-leaf parsley,
   chopped
5ml/1 tsp bicarbonate of soda
   (baking soda)
sunflower oil for deep-frying
sea salt and ground black pepper
lemon wedges, to serve

*Ideal street food, felafel are
one of the most popular
snacks in Lebanon, eaten
plain with pickles, or tucked
into pitta bread with onions
and yogurt.*

1 Drain the beans and chickpeas and place in a blender with the cumin and ground coriander. Blend to a thick purée, then add the chilli, onion, pepper, garlic and fresh herbs. Whizz until smooth – add a little water if necessary – and season with salt and pepper.

2 Transfer the paste to a bowl, add the bicarbonate of soda and beat well to combine. Cover the bowl with a cloth and leave for 15 minutes.

3 With wet hands, mould the mixture into small, tight balls. Heat enough oil for deep-frying in a pan and fry the balls in batches until golden brown. Drain the felafel on kitchen paper and serve warm, with lemon wedges to squeeze over them.

Spinach Pastries with Pine Nuts
Fatayer bil sabanikh

Serves 6

500g/1¼ lb fresh spinach, trimmed,
   washed and drained
30ml/2 tbsp olive oil, plus extra
   for brushing
15ml/1 tbsp butter
2 onions, chopped
45ml/3 tbsp pine nuts
15ml/1 tbsp ground sumac, or the
   juice of 1 lemon
5ml/1 tsp ground allspice
450g/1lb ready-prepared puff pastry
sea salt and ground black pepper

1 Steam the spinach until wilted, then drain, refresh under cold water and squeeze out the excess liquid. Chop the spinach coarsely.

2 Heat the oil and butter in a heavy pan and stir in the onion to soften. Add the pine nuts and cook for 2–3 minutes until the onions and pine nuts begin to turn golden. Stir in the spinach, sumac or lemon juice and allspice and season well. Remove from the heat.

3 Preheat the oven to 180°C/350°F/Gas 4. Roll out the pastry on a floured surface and cut out as many 10cm/4in rounds as you can. Spoon a little spinach mixture in the middle of each round and pull up the sides to make a pyramid by pinching the edges with your fingertips.

4 Line several baking trays with baking parchment and place the pastries on them. Brush the tops with a little oil and bake the pastries for about 30 minutes, until golden brown.

Variations of these pastries are found throughout the eastern Mediterranean; in Lebanon, they are often prepared by the Christian communities for Lent.

Lebanese Meat Pastries Sambousak bi lahma

Serves 6

30ml/2 tbsp olive oil
1 onion, finely chopped
30ml/2 tbsp pine nuts
250g/9oz lean lamb, finely minced
   (ground)
10ml/2 tsp ground cinnamon
30ml/2 tbsp thick, strained yogurt
small bunch of flat-leaf parsley,
   finely chopped
plain (all-purpose) flour, for dusting
450g/1lb ready-prepared puff pastry
sunflower oil, for frying
sea salt and ground black pepper

1 Heat the olive oil in a heavy pan, stir in the chopped onion and cook until transparent but not browned. Add the pine nuts to the onions and just as they begin to colour, stir in the minced lamb.

2 Cook the lamb mixture for 4–5 minutes until all the meat is browned, stirring constantly. Stir in the cinnamon and season well with salt and pepper. Transfer the mixture to a large bowl, and leave to cool, then beat in the strained yogurt and chopped parsley.

3 Dust the work surface with a little flour and roll out the puff pastry thinly. Cut into 10cm/4in rounds or squares, depending on whether you want to create half-moon shapes or triangles. Place 10ml/2 tsp of the meat mixture just off centre, then pull the other side of the pastry over the filling so that the edges touch.

4 Using your finger, dampen the edges with water and pinch together to seal. You can create a pattern along the edge with a fork, if you like.

5 Heat enough oil in a pan for deep-frying and fry the pastries in batches for 5–6 minutes, until they are golden brown. Drain on kitchen paper and serve warm or at room temperature.

Little meat pastries are popular throughout the eastern Mediterranean region, varying only in the spices and herbs employed or in the shape of the pastry – which may be half-moon shaped, triangular or cigar-shaped. Perhaps the most popular of all the pastries, these meat-filled ones grace many mezze tables in Lebanon and are prepared for celebratory feasts.

Sautéed Prawns with Coriander and Lime
Kreidess mikli

1 Heat the oil in a heavy pan, toss in the crushed garlic and cook, stirring constantly, until it begins to colour.

2 Add the lime rind, toss in the prawns, and stir-fry until they begin to turn pink.

3 Add the lime juice and fresh coriander and season with salt, and let the liquid sizzle before removing from the heat. Eat immediately with your fingers.

Serves 3–4

30–45ml/2–3 tbsp olive oil
2–3 cloves garlic, crushed
rind and juice of 1 lime
15–16 raw king prawns (jumbo shrimp), peeled to the tails and deveined
small bunch of fresh coriander (cilantro), roughly chopped
sea salt

Freshly caught large prawns cooked simply in this manner are delicious. There are many versions of this dish throughout the eastern Mediterranean, but this is served in the picturesque fishing villages up the coast from Beirut.

Poached Fish with Rice and Pine Nuts Sayadieh samak

1 Heat the oil in a heavy pan and fry the onions for 5–10 minutes, until dark brown. Turn off the heat and set aside.

2 Rub the fish with salt inside and out. Place the parsley leaves in the base of a pan, lay the fish on top and add the bay leaves, cinnamon stick and peppercorns. Just cover with water and bring to the boil. Reduce the heat and simmer gently for about 5 minutes. Transfer the fish to a board and leave it to cool a little, remove the skin, take the flesh off the bone and break into bitesize pieces. Cover with foil.

3 Return the skin, head and bones to the cooking liquid and bring to the boil. Reduce the heat and bubble for 15–20 minutes, to reduce by half. Strain the stock, return it to the pan and bring it to the boil.

4 Add the browned onions to the stock, and simmer for a further 10–15 minutes. Lift out the onions and press them through a sieve (strainer) back into the pot. Stir well and season. Return to the boil, add the rice, cumin and cinnamon and simmer for 10 minutes, until the rice has absorbed the stock. Turn off the heat, cover the pan with a clean dish towel, followed by the lid, and leave to steam for a further 10 minutes.

5 Turn the rice into a serving dish, stir a little of the fish into it and sprinkle the rest on top. Dry-roast the pine nuts in a pan until golden and sprinkle them over the top. Dust with cinnamon and serve with lemon wedges.

Serves 4–6

30–45ml/2–3 tbsp olive oil

2 onions, finely sliced

1 firm-fleshed fish, such as sea bass or trout (about 900g/2lb), scaled, gutted and cleaned

bunch of flat-leaf parsley

2–3 bay leaves

1 cinnamon stick

6 black peppercorns

250g/9oz/1¼ cups long grain rice, well rinsed and drained

5–10ml/1–2 tsp ground cumin

5–10ml/1–2 tsp ground cinnamon, plus extra for dusting

30ml/2 tbsp pine nuts

sea salt

1 lemon, cut into wedges, to serve

Originally a simple dish prepared by fishermen, this recipe has become more sophisticated and now ranks with the Lebanese classics. In restaurants in coastal areas it is often served as the plat du jour, whereas in homes it is prepared as a special dish to honour guests.

Charcoal-grilled Trout with Garlic, Lemon and Zahtar Samak meshwi

Serves 4

juice of 2 lemons
4 cloves garlic, crushed
4 small trout (about 300g/11oz
    each), gutted and cleaned
10ml/2 tsp zahtar
sea salt and ground pink
    peppercorns
1 lemon, cut into wedges, to serve

1 Prepare the barbecue (or preheat a ridged griddle). In a bowl, mix together the lemon juice and crushed garlic.

2 Using a sharp knife, score the flesh of the fish diagonally three times on each side. Rub a little salt and pepper into the fish, inside and out.

3 Brush one side of the fish with the lemon juice and place it, lemon-juice side down, on an oiled rack set over the glowing coals. Brush the rest of the lemon juice on the other side and grill the fish for about 4 minutes on each side.

4 Transfer the fish to a serving dish. Sprinkle the zahtar over the top and serve immediately with lemon wedges to squeeze over them.

The traditional method of cooking fish in the eastern Mediterranean is over charcoal or wood embers. Whether it is sea or freshwater fish, the flesh is always tasty and juicy cooked this way.

Fish with Tomato and Pomegranate Sauce
Tajin samak bi banadura

Serves 4

900g/2lb firm-fleshed fish fillets
45–60ml/3–4 tbsp olive oil
juice of 1 lemon
2–3 cloves garlic, finely chopped
4 tomatoes, skinned, seeded, and
    chopped
15ml/1 tbsp pomegranate molasses
10ml/2 tsp sugar
sea salt and ground black pepper
small bunch of fresh parsley, finely
    chopped, to garnish

This is a good way to cook any firm-fleshed fish, such as large sardines, sea bass, red snapper, grouper and trout. The pomegranate molasses adds a tangy, sour note to the sauce and enriches the colour. It is available from Middle Eastern stores and some specialist delicatessens and supermarkets.

1 Preheat the oven to 180°C/350°F/Gas 4. Arrange the fish in an ovenproof dish, rub with salt and pepper and pour over 30ml/2 tbsp olive oil and the lemon juice. Cover with foil and bake for about 25 minutes, until the fish is cooked.

2 Meanwhile, heat the rest of the oil in a heavy frying pan. Fry the garlic until it begins to colour, then add the tomatoes. Cook for 5 minutes, then stir in the pomegranate molasses with the sugar. Reduce the heat and cook gently until the sauce thickens. Season with salt and pepper. Keep warm until the fish is ready.

3 Arrange the fish on a serving dish, spoon the sauce over and around the fish and sprinkle with the parsley.

Serves 4–6

450g/1lb/2 cups finely minced
   (ground) lean lamb
1 onion, grated
10ml/2 tsp ground cinnamon
5ml/1 tsp ground cumin
5ml/1 tsp ground allspice
115g/4oz/⅔ cup fine bulgur, well
   rinsed and drained
30ml/2 tbsp olive oil, or melted ghee
sea salt and ground black pepper

For the topping

30–45ml/2–3 tbsp olive oil
2–3 onions, halved and sliced with
   the grain
30–45ml/2–3 tbsp pine nuts
5ml/1 tsp ground cinnamon
15ml/1 tbsp pomegranate molasses
sea salt and ground black pepper
15–30ml/1–2 tbsp light tahini and
   small bunch of fresh parsley, finely
   chopped, to serve

Baked Kibbeh with Onions and Pine Nuts Kibbeh saniyeh

1 Preheat the oven to 180°C/350°F/Gas 4 and grease a shallow ovenproof dish, such as a gratin dish or small roasting pan.

2 In a bowl, use a wooden spoon or your fists to pound the lamb with the onion and spices. Season with salt and pepper and knead well.

3 Add the bulgur to the lamb, and knead again for about 10 minutes, until the mixture is thoroughly mixed and has a paste-like consistency. Alternatively, you can place the mixture in a blender or food processor and whizz to a paste.

4 Turn the mixture into the greased dish and spread it evenly. Flatten the top with your knuckles and spread the oil or ghee over the surface. Using a sharp knife, cut the mixture into wedges or diamond shapes and bake in the oven for about 30 minutes, until nicely browned.

5 Meanwhile, make the topping. Heat the oil in a frying pan and cook the onions until they begin to brown. Add the pine nuts and stir until they turn golden. Add the cinnamon and pomegranate molasses and season with salt and pepper.

6 When the kibbeh is ready, spread the onion mixture over the top and return it to the oven for 5 minutes. Lift the portions on to a serving plate and drizzle the tahini over each one. Garnish with the parsley and serve while still warm.

There are numerous versions of kibbeh, which is one of Lebanon's treasured national dishes. Here, the kibbeh mixture is baked and topped with onions and pine nuts.

Pasha's Meatballs in Tomato Sauce Dawood Pasha

1 In a bowl, mix together the minced lamb, cinnamon and allspice and season with about 2.5ml/½ tsp salt and a good grinding of black pepper. Knead the mixture well with your hands then, with wet hands, mould it into small balls about the size of large cherries.

2 Heat enough sunflower oil for frying in a heavy pan. Roll the meatballs in a little flour and drop them into the oil. Fry for 4–5 minutes, turning, until they are nicely browned all over. Lift the meatballs out of the oil with a slotted spoon and drain them on kitchen paper.

3 To make the sauce, heat the ghee or olive oil and butter in a heavy pan and sauté the onions over a medium heat for 3–4 minutes, until golden brown. Stir in the pine nuts and cook until they begin to colour, then add the cinnamon, followed by the tomatoes and sugar.

4 Simmer the sauce, uncovered, for about 20 minutes, until it has reduced and thickened, and season with salt and pepper.

5 Place the meatballs in the sauce and heat through for 10 minutes. Serve hot with rice and lemon wedges.

This famous dish of meatballs cooked in a tomato sauce and served with rice is said to have been one of the favourite dishes of Dawood Pasha, the first governor of Mount Lebanon appointed by the Ottomans in 1860. The traditional recipe calls for the meat to be cooked in sheep's tail fat, but ghee, or olive oil with a knob of butter, is a practical substitute.

Serves 4
For the meatballs
450g/1lb/2 cups lean minced (ground) lamb
5–10ml/1–2 tsp ground cinnamon
5ml/1 tsp ground allspice
sunflower oil, for frying
plain (all-purpose) flour, for coating
sea salt and ground black pepper
1 lemon, cut into wedges, to serve
cooked rice and chopped fresh parsley, to accompany

For the sauce
15ml/1 tbsp ghee, or 15ml/1 tbsp olive oil with a knob of butter
2 onions, halved lengthways, cut in half crossways, and slice with the grain
30ml/2 tbsp pine nuts
5ml/1 tsp ground cinnamon
400g/14oz can chopped tomatoes
10ml/2 tsp sugar
sea salt and ground black pepper

Lamb Stew with Plums
Yakhnit al-khawkh

Serves 4–6

30ml/2 tbsp ghee, or 30ml/2 tbsp
   olive oil with a knob of butter
2 onions, finely chopped
2–3 cloves garlic, finely chopped
5ml/1 tsp ground cumin seeds
5ml/1 tsp ground coriander seeds
500g/1¼lb lean lamb, cut into cubes
plain (all-purpose) flour, for coating
400ml/14fl oz/1⅔ cups chicken
   stock
350g/12oz plums, stoned (pitted)
   and quartered
sea salt and ground black pepper
small bunch of fresh mint leaves,
   finely shredded, to garnish
plain pilaff, to serve

*A number of medieval
dishes incorporating meat
and fruit are still popular in
the eastern Mediterranean.
The most common include
lamb or chicken stewed with
apricots, prunes, quinces
and plums.*

1 Heat the ghee in a heavy pan and cook the onions until they begin to colour, then add the garlic, ground cumin and coriander seeds.

2 Toss the pieces of lamb in flour to coat them lightly, then add them to the pan to brown. Pour in the stock and bring it to the boil, reduce the heat, cover the pan and simmer for about 40 minutes.

3 Add the plums to the stew and season with salt and pepper. Cover the pan again and simmer for a further 20 minutes, or until the plums are tender.

4 Transfer the stew to a warmed serving dish, garnish with the shredded mint, and serve with a plain, buttery pilaff.

Aromatic Chicken on Toasted Pitta Bread
Shawarma dajaj

Serves 4

4 chicken breasts
sea salt
4 pitta breads
tahini sauce and pickled vegetables,
    to serve

For the marinade

30–45ml/2–3 tbsp olive oil
juice of 2–3 lemons
10ml/2 tsp white wine or cider
    vinegar
2 cloves garlic, crushed
1 cinnamon stick, broken into pieces
grated rind of ½ orange
4–6 cardamom pods, crushed
ground black pepper

The shawarma dishes of Lebanon are the equivalent of the Turkish döner kebab and are popular street food. When made with chicken, it is marinated first in a deliciously aromatic combination of spices and served in pitta bread.

1 Mix together the ingredients for the marinade and toss the chicken breasts in the mixture, then cover and leave in the refrigerator to marinate for at least 6 hours.

2 Preheat the oven to 180°C/350°F/Gas 4. Lay the chicken in an ovenproof dish, baste with the marinade, and place in the oven for about 20 minutes.

3 Lift out the chicken and slice it finely, then return it to the dish. Baste with the cooking juices, season with salt, and return to the oven for a further 10 minutes.

4 Place the pitta breads on an oven tray and toast them in the oven for 5 minutes. Serve the chicken in the pitta pouches, or on top of the pitta bread, and accompany with a tahini sauce and pickled vegetables.

Stuffed Artichoke Bottoms Ardishawk bil lahma

Serves 4

30ml/2 tbsp olive oil
2 medium onions, finely chopped
15–30ml/1–2 tbsp pine nuts
350g/12oz/1½ cups lean minced (ground) lamb
5ml/1 tsp ground cinnamon
2.5ml/½ tsp ground allspice
4–6 fresh (see cook's tip) or frozen artichoke bottoms
juice of 1 lemon
200ml/7fl oz/scant 1 cup water
15ml/1 tbsp plain (all-purpose) flour
sea salt and ground black pepper
1 lemon, cut into wedges, to serve

1 Preheat the oven to 180°C/350°F/Gas 4. Heat the oil in a heavy pan and cook the onions for 2–3 minutes until they begin to colour.

2 Stir in the pine nuts, reserving a few for garnishing, and cook for 1–2 minutes until they turn golden, then add the lamb and spices and fry until the lamb begins to brown. Season with salt and pepper.

3 Place the artichoke bottoms, side by side, in a shallow ovenproof dish. Using a spoon, fill the artichokes with the meat mixture.

4 Combine the lemon juice and water in a bowl and stir in the flour, making sure it is thoroughly blended, then pour the mixture over the artichokes.

5 Cover the dish with foil and place it in the oven for 25–30 minutes, until the artichokes are tender. Meanwhile, heat a frying pan and dry-roast the reserved pine nuts until golden brown.

6 Remove the stuffed artichokes from the oven and transfer to a warmed serving dish. Sprinkle the roasted pine nuts over the top of the artichokes and serve with wedges of lemon to squeeze over them.

COOK'S TIP

Fresh artichokes should be treated like flowers and kept with their stems in water until ready to use. To prepare them for this dish, pull off the outer leaves, cut off the stalks and slice away the purple choke, the small leaves and any hard bits. Remove any fibres with the edge of a spoon and rub the artichoke bottoms with a mixture of lemon juice and salt to prevent them from discolouring.

When globe artichokes are in season, you will find this dish being prepared in homes throughout the eastern Mediterranean region.

Roasted Green Wheat with Chillies and Pistachios Frikkeh

1 Heat the ghee, or olive oil and butter mixture, in a heavy pan and stir in the sliced onion, garlic and chillies. Cook until they begin to colour. Add the halved pistachios to the pan and fry for 1 minute, then stir in the frikkeh, coating it in the butter.

2 Pour in enough stock to just cover the mixture and bring it to the boil. Add salt and pepper to taste, reduce the heat and simmer for 15–20 minutes, until all the stock has been absorbed. Turn off the heat, cover the pan with a clean dish towel, followed by the lid, and leave the grains to steam for a further 10 minutes.

3 Meanwhile, put the pine nuts in a frying pan and dry-roast them over a medium heat, until golden brown. Remove from the heat and turn out on to a plate.

4 Turn the frikkeh into a warmed serving dish and sprinkle the pine nuts over the top. Serve immediately, with a dollop of creamy yogurt, as an accompaniment to any roasted or barbecued meat or poultry dish.

COOK'S TIP
An ancient food in Arab cuisine, frikkeh is highly nutritious, very high in fibre and with a low GI rating. Look for frikkeh in Middle Eastern and health food stores.

Serves 4–6
30ml/2 tbsp ghee or 30ml/2 tbsp
 olive oil with a knob of butter
1 onion, finely sliced
2 cloves garlic, finely chopped
1–2 green chillies, seeded and finely
 sliced
115g/4oz/1 cup unsalted pistachios,
 halved
250g/9oz frikkeh, rinsed
900ml/1½ pints/3¾ cups well-
 flavoured chicken stock
30ml/2 tbsp pine nuts
sea salt and ground black pepper
creamy yogurt, to serve

Also known as freek, frikkeh is immature wheat that has been roasted in the husk to produce grain with a nutty texture and a mild smoky flavour. The green grains are cooked like ordinary wheat grains and served on their own or as an accompaniment to a main dish.

Green Lentils with Bulgur Imjadra

Serves 4–6

225g/8oz/1 cup green lentils, rinsed
30ml/2 tbsp ghee, or olive oil with a
   knob of butter
2 onions, finely chopped
5–10ml/1–2 tsp cumin seeds
225g/8oz/1¼ cups coarse bulgur,
   rinsed
900ml/1½ pints/3¾ cups stock or
   water
sea salt and ground black pepper

To serve

15ml/1 tbsp ghee or butter
small bunch of fresh coriander
   (cilantro), coarsely chopped
small bunch of mint, coarsely
   chopped

*This delicious side salad is
one of Lebanon's lesser
known countryside
specialities. It combines
lentils with a grain to
produce a wholesome dish
that can be served on its
own, or with any meat,
poultry or fish dish.*

1 Bring a pan of water to the boil, add the lentils and cook for about 15 minutes, until they are tender but not soft or mushy. Drain and refresh under cold water.

2 Heat the ghee in a heavy pan, stir in the onions and cook until it begins to colour. Add the cumin seeds and stir in the bulgur, coating it in the ghee. Stir in the lentils and pour in the stock.

3 Season with salt and pepper and bring to the boil. Reduce the heat and simmer for 15 minutes. Turn off the heat and place a clean dish towel over the pan, followed by the lid. Leave the bulgur and lentils to steam for 10 minutes.

4 Meanwhile, melt the butter in a small pan. Turn the rice and lentils into a serving dish, pour the melted butter over the top and garnish with the coriander and mint.

Butter Bean Stew Fassoulia baida

Serves 4–6

450/1lb/2½ cups dried butter (lima)
   beans, soaked overnight
30ml/2 tbsp olive oil with a knob of
   butter, or 30ml/2 tbsp ghee
2 onions, finely chopped
4–6 cloves garlic, crushed
10ml/2 tsp sugar
10ml/2 tsp ground cumin seeds
10ml/2 tsp ground coriander seeds
1 large cinnamon stick
2 x 400g/14oz cans chopped
   tomatoes
small bunch of fresh coriander
   (cilantro), coarsely chopped
sea salt and ground black pepper

*As beans are cheap,
nourishing and readily
available, there are times
when a stew like this may
constitute the main meal of
the day. Some include meat
or root vegetables, but this
version simply contains
beans and is best served
with a dollop of yogurt and
bread to mop up the sauce.*

1 Drain the beans and transfer them into a pan filled with water. Bring to the boil, reduce the heat and simmer the beans for about 45 minutes, until tender but retaining a bite. Drain, refresh in cold water, and remove any loose skins.

2 Heat the oil and butter in a heavy pan and cook the onions, garlic and sugar for 2–3 minutes, until they begin to colour. Add the spices and toss in the beans. Add the tomatoes and cook over a medium heat for about 20 minutes.

3 Season the stew with salt and pepper and stir in half the fresh coriander. Remove the cinnamon and transfer the beans into a serving bowl. Garnish with the remaining coriander and serve with bread, or as an accompaniment to a meat or grain dish.

Stuffed Aubergines in Oil Batinjan bi zeit

Serves 4–6
150ml/¼ pint/⅔ cup olive oil
1 onion, finely chopped
2 tomatoes, skinned, seeded and
    chopped
10ml/2 tsp sabaa baharat
10ml/2 tsp dried mint
5–10ml/1–2 tsp sugar
175g/6oz/¾ cup short grain rice
6 medium slim aubergines
    (eggplants)
1–2 small potatoes, sliced
juice of 1 lemon
sea salt and ground black pepper

1 To make the stuffing, heat 15ml/1 tbsp of the olive oil in a heavy pan and cook the onion for 2–3 minutes until it begins to colour. Add the tomatoes, spice mix, mint and a little sugar and cook for 2–3 minutes.

2 Add the rice to the pan, coating it well in the oil, and pour in enough water to cover the rice by a finger's width. Season and bring to the boil. Reduce the heat and simmer for 10 minutes, until all the water has been absorbed. Turn off the heat, cover the pan with a clean dish towel and put on the lid. Leave the rice to steam for 10 minutes.

3 Meanwhile, prepare the aubergines. Cut off the stalks and use an apple corer to hollow out the middle, or pummel the aubergines with your fingers to loosen the flesh from the skin and squeeze out the flesh through the opening at the stalk end.

4 Fill each aubergine with the rice mixture and seal the opening with a slice of potato. Stand the aubergines in a heavy pan.

5 Mix the lemon juice and remaining olive oil with 100ml/3½fl oz/scant ½ cup water and pour it around the aubergines. Bring to the boil, reduce the heat, cover the pan and simmer for about 40 minutes. Serve hot or at room temperature.

There are many variations of stuffed vegetable dishes throughout the eastern Mediterranean region. In Lebanon, the local spice mix, sabaa baharat, *which is a blend of seven spices, is often used to flavour the rice filling in this dish, but if you cannot find it you can just use a combination of ground cumin, coriander and cinnamon. Serve these stuffed aubergines as an accompaniment to any roast fish or meat, or on their own as an appetizer.*

Spicy Potatoes with Coriander Batata harra

Serves 4

350g/12oz new potatoes
60ml/4 tbsp olive oil or 30ml/2 tbsp
   ghee
3–4 cloves garlic, finely chopped
2 red chillies, seeded and finely
   chopped
5–10ml/1–2 tsp ground cumin seeds
bunch of fresh coriander (cilantro),
   finely chopped
sea salt and ground black pepper
1 lemon, cut into wedges, to serve

The spices in this popular potato dish vary across Lebanon, Syria and Jordan but the recipes invariably include chillies and cumin. The dish can be eaten at room temperature as part of a mezze spread, but is also often served hot as an accompaniment to grilled and roasted meat and fish.

1 Steam the potatoes with their skins on for about 10 minutes, until they are cooked but still firm. Drain them and refresh under cold running water. Peel off the skins and cut the potatoes into bitesize pieces.

2 Heat the oil or ghee in a heavy pan and cook the garlic, chillies and cumin seeds for 2–3 minutes, until they begin to colour. Add the potatoes, turning them to make sure they are coated in the oil and spices, and fry for about 5 minutes.

3 Season the potatoes with salt and pepper and stir in most of the coriander. (If serving the dish at room temperature, leave the potatoes to cool first.) Sprinkle the remaining coriander over the top and serve the potatoes from the pan with lemon wedges to squeeze over them.

Roasted Courgettes with Vinegar Koussa bil khal

Serves 4–6

4–6 courgettes (zucchini), trimmed and sliced lengthways
4 cloves garlic, halved and lightly crushed
45–60ml/3–4 tbsp olive oil
30ml/2 tbsp cider or white wine vinegar
10ml/2 tsp dried mint
sea salt

1 Preheat the oven to 180°C/350°F/Gas 4. Place the courgette slices in an ovenproof dish with the garlic cloves.

2 Pour the olive oil over the courgettes, and roast in the oven for 25–30 minutes, until softened and lightly browned.

3 Lift the courgette slices and some of the garlic out of the dish and arrange on a warmed serving plate.

4 Mix 30–45ml/2–3 tbsp of the cooking oil with the vinegar and dried mint and drizzle it over the courgettes. Sprinkle with salt and serve warm or at room temperature.

The courgette is a very popular vegetable in the eastern Mediterranean region, and in the markets you can find marbled green courgettes and white ones as well as the more usual green type. Any kind will do for this recipe, which makes a lovely side dish for grilled or roasted meats and fish.

Spinach with Yogurt
Fattet al sabanekh

1 To prepare the yogurt sauce, beat the yogurt with the garlic, tahini and lemon juice and season it to taste with salt and pepper. Set aside.

2 Put the spinach in a steamer or a large pan and cook briefly until just wilted. Refresh under cold running water, drain and squeeze out the excess water. Chop the spinach coarsely.

3 Heat the oil in a heavy pan, stir in the onion and cook for 2–3 minutes. Stir in the ground spices and then add the spinach, making sure all the leaves are thoroughly mixed with the spiced oil. Cook for a further 2–3 minutes, until the spinach is wilted. Season well with salt and pepper. Mix in the fresh coriander and flaked almonds.

4 Break the toasted pitta bread into bitesize pieces and arrange them in a serving dish. Spread the spinach over the top of the bread and spoon the yogurt sauce over the spinach.

5 Quickly melt the butter in a frying pan and add the pine nuts. Stir-fry until the pine nuts are golden in colour. Drizzle the butter from the pan over the yogurt and sprinkle the pine nuts on top. Serve immediately while the spinach is still warm.

Serves 4

500g/1¼lb fresh spinach, washed and drained
15–30ml/1–2 tbsp olive oil
1 onion, chopped
5ml/1 tsp ground cinnamon
5ml/1 tsp paprika
5ml/1 tsp ground cumin
small bunch of fresh coriander (cilantro), finely chopped
15–30ml/1–2 tbsp flaked (sliced) almonds
2 pitta breads, toasted
15ml/1 tbsp butter
15–30ml/1–2 tbsp pine nuts
sea salt and ground black pepper

For the yogurt sauce

600ml/1 pint/2½ cups creamy, strained yogurt
2 cloves garlic, crushed
30ml/2 tbsp tahini
juice of ½ lemon
sea salt and ground black pepper

As with all traditional fatta dishes, which were probably devised as a way of using up stale bread, the spinach is served on toasted flat bread and topped with melted butter and pine nuts.

Cream Cheese Pudding with Syrup and Nuts Ashtalieh

1 Heat the milk in a heavy pan with the sugar, stirring all the time, and bring it to the boil. Reduce the heat and add the cream cheese, beating it into the milk and sugar until the mixture is smooth.

2 Add a couple of spoonfuls of the hot mixture to the slaked rice flour or cornflour, then pour it into the pan, whisking vigorously until the mixture thickens.

3 Stir in the orange blossom water, and simmer gently for 10–15 minutes until it is very thick. Pour the mixture into a shallow dish and leave it to cool and set. Chill in the refrigerator until ready to use.

4 To make the syrup, put the sugar in a heavy-based pan with 120ml/4fl oz/½ cup water and bring it to the boil, stirring constantly until the sugar has dissolved.

5 Add the lemon juice and rind, reduce the heat and simmer for 10 minutes, until the syrup is thick enough to coat the back of a spoon. Remove from the heat and leave the syrup to cool.

6 When ready to serve, divide the pudding into squares and place them on individual plates. Spoon some of the syrup over them and decorate with the nuts. Serve chilled or at room temperature.

Serves 4–6

1 litre/1¾ pints/4 cups full-fat milk
60ml/4 tbsp sugar
250g/9oz/generous 1 cup cream cheese
90ml/6 tbsp rice flour or cornflour (cornstarch), mixed with a little extra milk
10–15ml/2–3 tsp orange blossom water
15ml/1 tbsp pine nuts, soaked in cold water overnight
30ml/2 tbsp blanched almonds, soaked in cold water overnight and cut into slivers
30ml/2 tbsp pistachio nuts, chopped

For the syrup

225g/8oz/1 generous cup sugar
juice of 1 lemon
rind of ½ lemon, cut into fine strips

This cream cheese pudding is similar to the classic milk pudding, although thicker and creamier so that it can be cut into squares, which are then bathed in the traditional sugar syrup, kater. The pudding is invariably decorated with chopped pistachio nuts, almonds and pine nuts, which are soaked overnight to soften and refresh them.

Serves 6–8
For the semolina
600ml/1 pint/2½ cups whole milk
60ml/4 tbsp sugar
90g/3½oz/½ cup fine semolina
1–2 mastic crystals, pulverized with a
    little sugar

For the cream
15ml/1 tbsp rice flour
150ml/¼ pint/⅔ cup whole milk
300ml/½ pint/1¼ cups double
    (heavy) cream
30–45ml/2–3 tbsp sugar
2 slices white bread, ground to
    crumbs
15ml/1 tbsp rose water

For the topping
2 bananas, finely sliced
juice of ½ lemon
30ml/2 tbsp chopped pistachio nuts
30ml/2 tbsp flaked almonds
45–60ml/3–4 tbsp fragrant runny
    honey
30ml/2 tbsp orange blossom water

Nights of Lebanon
Layali loubnan

1 First prepare the semolina. Heat the milk with the sugar in a heavy pan, stirring until the sugar has dissolved. Bring the milk to the boil, then add in the semolina and the mastic, beating vigorously. Reduce the heat and simmer, stirring from time to time, until the mixture thickens. Pour it into a serving dish, level it with the back of a spoon and leave to cool.

2 To prepare the cream layer, mix the rice flour with a little milk, heat the rest of the milk and cream, together with the sugar, stirring constantly, until almost boiling. Stir a spoonful of the hot mixture into the rice flour mixture and then pour the rice flour mixture back into the pan.

3 Add the breadcrumbs and rose water to the pan and stir vigorously until the mixture is thick and creamy. Leave to cool a little, then spoon it over the semolina, which should have set. Leave to cool and set, then chill the pudding.

4 A little time before serving, arrange the sliced bananas in a layer over the pudding. Squeeze lemon juice over the top to prevent them from turning brown. Sprinkle the nuts on top. Heat the honey with the orange blossom water and pour it over the nuts. Once the honey has cooled, chill the pudding until ready to eat.

This pudding is often made for family celebrations and can be made ahead of time. Traditionally, it has a layer of semolina, followed by a layer of kashta (a scented creamy mixture), topped by a layer of bananas, and finished with nuts, but it can include additional ingredients, such as apricot, cherry or rose petal conserves. The whole pudding is drizzled in amber honey and orange blossom water.

Wheat in Fragrant Honey Kamhiyeh

Serves 6

225g/8oz/1¼ cups whole wheat
  grains, soaked overnight and
  drained
1 litre/1¾ pints/4 cups water
60–90ml/4–6 tbsp runny honey
30ml/2 tbsp orange blossom water
30ml/2 tbsp rose water
30–45ml/2–3 tbsp raisins or
  sultanas (golden raisins), soaked
  in warm water for 30 minutes and
  drained
30ml/2 tbsp pine nuts, soaked in
  water for 2 hours
30ml/2 tbsp blanched almonds,
  soaked in water for 2 hours
seeds of ½ pomegranate

*This dessert is prepared
with young green wheat or
barley to mark significant
events. For Muslims, it is a
dish prepared for nursing
mothers; Jews serve it to
celebrate a baby's first
tooth; and for Christians,
it is eaten on 4 December
in honour of St Barbara.*

1 Place the whole wheat grains in a heavy pan with the water and bring to the boil. Reduce the heat, cover, and simmer for about 1 hour, until the grains are tender and most of the water has been absorbed.

2 Meanwhile, heat the honey and stir in the orange blossom and rose waters – don't let it bubble up. Stir in the raisins and turn off the heat.

3 Transfer the wheat grains into a serving bowl, or individual bowls, and pour the honey and raisins over the top. Garnish with the nuts and pomegranate seeds and serve while still warm, or leave to cool and chill in the refrigerator before serving.

Stuffed Red Date Preserve Mrabba al-balah

Makes enough for 2 x 450g/1lb jars
40 fresh, ripe red dates
40 blanched whole almonds
500g/1¼lb/2½ cups sugar
juice and rind (cut into fine strips) of
    2 clementines
6–8 cloves

This is a beautiful and unusual preserve, revered in Lebanon and Jordan. Dates are one of the region's most ancient staple foods, coveted for their nutritional value and their sweetness. It is said that the Bedouin cannot sleep under fruit-laden date palms, such is their urge to pick and devour the fruit. It will keep in sterilized jars for up to 3 months.

1 Place the dates in a heavy pan and just cover with water. Bring to the boil, reduce the heat and simmer for 5 minutes to soften the dates. Drain the dates, reserving the water, and carefully push the stone (pit) out of each date with a skewer or a sharp knife. Stuff each date with an almond.

2 Pour the reserved cooking water back into the pan and add the sugar, clementine juice and rind, and the cloves. Bring the water to the boil, stirring constantly until the sugar has dissolved.

3 Reduce the heat and drop in the stuffed dates. Simmer for about 1 hour, until the syrup is fairly thick. Leave the dates to cool in the syrup, then spoon them into jars to enjoy with bread, yogurt, milk puddings, or just as a treat on their own.

Lebanese Coffee with Cardamom
Kahwe Lebananieh

Serves 2

20ml/4 heaped tsp finely ground
   coffee
seeds of 2–3 cardamom pods,
   ground
10ml/2 tsp sugar, or more to taste

Lebanese coffee is very similar to the better-known Turkish coffee, although it is traditionally flavoured with cardamom. You can buy the finely ground coffee required to make it in Middle Eastern stores and delicatessens. It is prepared in a distinctive long-handled pot, known as a rakweh in Lebanon, and is generally served black and already sweetened.

1 Put two coffee-cupfuls of water into the rakweh, or a small pot, and heap the coffee, cardamom and sugar on the surface. Place on the heat. As the water begins to boil, stir the coffee into the water. Allow to bubble for 2–3 minutes, stirring constantly, then pour the coffee into warmed coffee cups.

2 Serve immediately, but let the coffee sit for a moment before drinking, so that the grounds sink to the bottom of the cup.

COOK'S TIP

To grind the cardamom pods, simply crush the pods in a mortar and pestle, or on a wooden board with the flat side of a heavy, bladed knife. You want to split them rather than grind them to dust.

Nutritional notes

Fried Halloumi with Zahtar: Energy 328kcal/1356kJ; Protein 16.2g; Carbohydrate 1.7g, of which sugars 0g; Fat 28.6g, of which saturates 13.1g; Cholesterol 48mg; Calcium 311mg; Fibre 0g; Sodium 331mg

Smoked Aubergine Dip: Energy 91kcal/375kJ; Protein 1g; Carbohydrate 2.2g, of which sugars 1.5g; Fat 8.8g, of which saturates 1.4g; Cholesterol 8mg; Calcium 8mg; Fibre 1.4g; Sodium 52mg

Chickpea and Bulgur Salad with Mint: Energy 267kcal/1116kJ; Protein 8.6g; Carbohydrate 34.1g, of which sugars 3.3g; Fat 11.4g, of which saturates 1.4g; Cholesterol 0mg; Calcium 89mg; Fibre 4.1g; Sodium 153mg

Chicken Wings with Garlic and Sumac: Energy 272kcal/1132kJ; Protein 23g; Carbohydrate 1.4g, of which sugars 0.1g; Fat 19.5g, of which saturates 4.7g; Cholesterol 98mg; Calcium 12mg; Fibre 0.1g; Sodium 68mg

Chicken and Saffron Broth with Noodles: Energy 260kcal/1088kJ; Protein 28.4g; Carbohydrate 11.3g, of which sugars 0g; Fat 11.3g, of which saturates 3.4g; Cholesterol 86mg; Calcium 17mg; Fibre 0g; Sodium 106mg

Creamy Red Lentil Soup with Cumin: Energy 235kcal/991kJ; Protein 13g; Carbohydrate 28.4g, of which sugars 3.7g; Fat 8.9g, of which saturates 2.2g; Cholesterol 0mg; Calcium 66mg; Fibre 2.9g; Sodium 40mg

Little Flat Breads with Thyme and Sumac: Energy 310kcal/1314kJ; Protein 8.2g; Carbohydrate 60.9g, of which sugars 1.1g; Fat 5.6g, of which saturates 0.8g; Cholesterol 0mg; Calcium 119mg; Fibre 2.3g; Sodium 169mg

Spicy Bean Balls: Energy 303kcal/1282kJ; Protein 18.5g; Carbohydrate 44.7g, of which sugars 5.2g; Fat 6.9g, of which saturates 1.2g; Cholesterol 0mg; Calcium 88mg; Fibre 7.2g; Sodium 16mg

Spinach Pastries with Pine Nuts: Energy 441kcal/1834kJ; Protein 9g; Carbohydrate 36.8g, of which sugars 7.2g; Fat 30.4g, of which saturates 2.3g; Cholesterol 6mg; Calcium 212mg; Fibre 3.1g; Sodium 371mg

Lebanese Meat Pastries: Energy 555kcal/2308kJ; Protein 14.5g; Carbohydrate 34.8g, of which sugars 4.4g; Fat 41.5g, of which saturates 4.3g; Cholesterol 32mg; Calcium 76mg; Fibre 0.9g; Sodium 275mg

Sautéed Prawns with Coriander and Lime: Energy 106kcal/442kJ; Protein 11.8g; Carbohydrate 1.2g, of which sugars 0.4g; Fat 6.1g, of which saturates 0.9g; Cholesterol 122mg; Calcium 75mg; Fibre 0.8g; Sodium 123mg

Poached Fish with Rice and Pine Nuts: Energy 385kcal/1611kJ; Protein 28.3g; Carbohydrate 40.6g, of which sugars 4.9g; Fat 12.2g, of which saturates 1.8g; Cholesterol 96mg; Calcium 68mg; Fibre 1.3g; Sodium 90mg

Charcoal-grilled Trout with Garlic, Lemon and Zahtar: Energy 279kcal/1176kJ; Protein 47.3g; Carbohydrate 1.7g, of which sugars 0.1g; Fat 9.4g, of which saturates 2.2g; Cholesterol 192mg; Calcium 78mg; Fibre 0.2g; Sodium 175mg

Fish with Tomato and Pomegranate Sauce: Energy 284kcal/1192kJ; Protein 41.7g; Carbohydrate 6.9g, of which sugars 6.9g; Fat 10.1g, of which saturates 1.5g; Cholesterol 104mg; Calcium 28mg; Fibre 0.8g; Sodium 149mg

Baked Kibbeh with Onions and Pine Nuts: Energy 399kcal/1659kJ; Protein 20.6g; Carbohydrate 30.4g, of which sugars 9.6g; Fat 22.4g, of which saturates 5.4g; Cholesterol 57mg; Calcium 69mg; Fibre 2.5g; Sodium 73mg

Pasha's Meatballs in Tomato Sauce: Energy 485kcal/2014kJ; Protein 25.4g; Carbohydrate 18.1g, of which sugars 11.7g; Fat 35.2g, of which saturates 10.9g; Cholesterol 95mg; Calcium 66mg; Fibre 2.7g; Sodium 119mg

Lamb Stew with Plums: Energy 262kcal/1092kJ; Protein 18.4g; Carbohydrate 14.3g, of which sugars 9.6g; Fat 15g, of which saturates 6.7g; Cholesterol 63mg; Calcium 44mg; Fibre 2.1g; Sodium 212mg

Aromatic Chicken on Toasted Pitta Bread: Energy 408kcal/1726kJ; Protein 40.2g; Carbohydrate 44.7g, of which sugars 1.8g; Fat 8.9g, of which saturates 2.1g; Cholesterol 65mg; Calcium 90mg; Fibre 1.7g; Sodium 499mg

Stuffed Artichoke Bottoms: Energy 277kcal/1153kJ; Protein 19.7g; Carbohydrate 14.3g, of which sugars 7.3g; Fat 16.1g, of which saturates 5.4g; Cholesterol 67mg; Calcium 61mg; Fibre 2.2g; Sodium 96mg

Roasted Green Wheat with Chillies and Pistachios: Energy 342kcal/1420kJ; Protein 8.7g; Carbohydrate 36.2g, of which sugars 3.2g; Fat 18.6g, of which saturates 2.2g; Cholesterol 0mg; Calcium 49mg; Fibre 1.7g; Sodium 226mg

Green Lentils with Bulgur: Energy 306kcal/1284kJ; Protein 13.8g; Carbohydrate 52.8g, of which sugars 4.2g; Fat 5.4g, of which saturates 0.6g; Cholesterol 0mg; Calcium 63mg; Fibre 4.3g; Sodium 9mg

Butter Bean Stew: Energy 295kcal/1251kJ; Protein 18.8g; Carbohydrate 45.4g, of which sugars 11.5g; Fat 5.7g, of which saturates 0.9g; Cholesterol 0mg; Calcium 108mg; Fibre 14.1g; Sodium 29mg

Stuffed Aubergines in Oil: Energy 486kcal/2023kJ; Protein 10.8g; Carbohydrate 76.2g, of which sugars 34.9g; Fat 16.8g, of which saturates 2.3g; Cholesterol 0mg; Calcium 160mg; Fibre 10.8g; Sodium 26mg

Spicy Potatoes with Coriander: Energy 174kcal/723kJ; Protein 2.4g; Carbohydrate 15.5g, of which sugars 1.2g; Fat 11.8g, of which saturates 1.7g; Cholesterol 0mg; Calcium 16mg; Fibre 0.9g; Sodium 12mg

Roasted Courgettes with Vinegar: Energy 78kcal/322kJ; Protein 2.7g; Carbohydrate 3.3g, of which sugars 2.1g; Fat 6g, of which saturates 0.9g; Cholesterol 0mg; Calcium 36mg; Fibre 1.3g; Sodium 2mg

Spinach with Yogurt: Energy 435kcal/1818kJ; Protein 19.3g; Carbohydrate 45.1g, of which sugars 20g; Fat 21.3g, of which saturates 4.8g; Cholesterol 11mg; Calcium 625mg; Fibre 5.9g; Sodium 529mg

Cream Cheese Pudding with Syrup and Nuts: Energy 613kcal/2561kJ; Protein 10.1g; Carbohydrate 70.5g, of which sugars 58.2g; Fat 33.7g, of which saturates 17.1g; Cholesterol 63mg; Calcium 279mg; Fibre 1g; Sodium 248mg

Nights of Lebanon: Energy 431kcal/1799kJ; Protein 7.5g; Carbohydrate 43.5g, of which sugars 27.8g; Fat 28.4g, of which saturates 14g; Cholesterol 62mg; Calcium 158mg; Fibre 1.2g; Sodium 124mg

Wheat in Fragrant Honey: Energy 193kcal/806kJ; Protein 4.1g; Carbohydrate 30.9g, of which sugars 11.5g; Fat 6.6g, of which saturates 0.5g; Cholesterol 0mg; Calcium 23mg; Fibre 0.6g; Sodium 3mg

Stuffed Red Date Preserve: Energy 1619kcal/6871kJ; Protein 15.8g; Carbohydrate 347.4g, of which sugars 346g; Fat 28.2g, of which saturates 2.4g; Cholesterol 0mg; Calcium 318mg; Fibre 8.3g; Sodium 45mg

Lebanese Coffee with Cardamom: Energy 22kcal/92kJ; Protein 0.3g; Carbohydrate 5.5g, of which sugars 5.2g; Fat 0g, of which saturates 0g; Cholesterol 0mg; Calcium 6mg; Fibre 0g; Sodium 1mg

Index

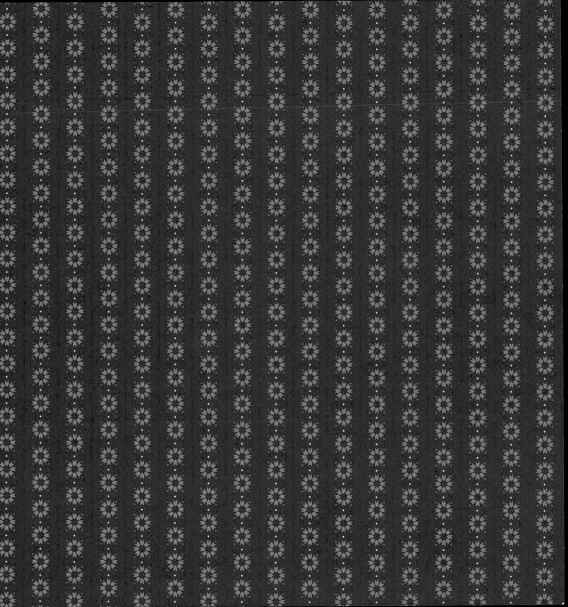